25 Things
a 16-Year-Old
Should Know

Patrick McIvor

DEDICATION

For Leah, Emma and Claire

FOREWORD

By Rodney Cutler

I've worked with Patrick McIvor since the early 1990s, and it has always fascinated me that regardless of the highs and lows or twists and turns in both his personal and professional life, he has the unique ability to block out the rearview mirror and focus on the road ahead. Patrick is an amazing family man and a loyal friend with an unlimited amount of energy. He has an extraordinary talent for connecting with people in an instant—whether on stage with a large audience or one-on-one in a meeting—and he uses that talent to bring his experiences to life in the pages of this book.

Patrick's wild curiosity for answers drives him to find solutions to any problem, and whenever I'm fortunate enough to spend a day with him I always learn something new. Reading this book is a lot like spending a day in Patrick's company, and I'm confident that you will come away with lots of new ideas for creating a life you love.

Rodney Cutler is founder of Cutler Salons in New York City where he has collaborated with designers for NY Fashion Week and offered men's grooming advice as a columnist for Esquire.

CONTENTS

Section One: Three Keys to Success

#1 The Five People They Hang Out With Are Better Than Them

#2 They Travel

#3 They Create Their Jobs/Success

Section Two: Three Keys to Financial Success

#4 They Understand There Are Only 100 Pennies In Every Dollar

#5 They Understand the Difference Between an Expense and an Investment, Including The Difference Between Good Debt and Bad Debt

#6 They Understand You Can't Live on Tomorrow, But You Can Build on Today

Section Three: 19 Things I Learned Along The Way

#7 Experience is the Ability to Recognize a Mistake When I Am About to Make It AGAIN

#8 I'm Not That Special

#9 Never Be A Consideration, Always Be a Yes or No

#10 Create an Experience

#11 If You Are Not Crashing You Are Not Going Fast Enough

#12 Excuses Are For Losers

CONTENTS continue

#13 You Can't Plan a Good Bank Robbery When You Are Too Busy Robbing Gas Stations

#14 Money Is a Tool, Not Something You Spend

#15 Know Your Brand

#16 Be Innovative or Don't Let Your Groove Turn Into a Rut

#17 Being the Best Doesn't Even Count

#18 It Is Not Important What You Do; What's Important is That You Can DO Something Better Than Others

#19 Be Professional, Always

#20 Ready, Fire, Aim

#21 Figure Out What You Have to Do in Order to Do What You Want To Do

#22 Don't Be NICE, Be Honest

#23 Nine Times Out Of Ten the Problem is Me

#24 Be 100% Committed

#25 There Ain't No Traffic On The Extra Mile

ACKNOWLEDGMENTS

I couldn't have written this book without the encouragement and support of my wife Leah. Meeting Leah when I was 24 and she was just 18 was a turning point in my life. She is the glue that holds our family together, and I cannot thank her enough for holding down the fort while I was on the road 200 days out of the year. I can count on her to tell me when one of my crazy ideas is just that— too crazy. I can also count on her to give me the courage to give it my all when she thinks that one of my crazy ideas just might work. Her stability and support mean the world to me, and I am eternally grateful that she has been willing to put up with me for nearly 30 years while we've been on this extraordinary journey together. My daughters, Emma and Claire, are a constant source of inspiration to me as I watch them create meaningful lives for themselves, and I wrote this book to share what I've learned with them. I also want to thank my parents, Judy and Patrick McIvor, who literally told me to "go for it" for as long as I can remember. I know I was a handful growing up, but they never lost faith in me. I also owe a great deal to my best friend, Rodney Cutler, and Pierre Villageville and Louise Stewart—three people I hold myself accountable to every day because of the lessons I learned from them. Finally, I'd like to thank Marianne Dougherty, who not only published my first professionally credited photograph but also believed in me enough to shepherd this book to publication.

INTRODUCTION

I have been very lucky in my life, stumbling from opportunity to opportunity with many chances to learn along the way. There have been moments when something happened or someone said something that put me on a direct path to success. One such moment happened on a trip I took to New York City with my oldest daughter, Emma, for a speaking engagement at an international beauty show at the Jacob Javits Convention Center. Some of the world's top stylists and even a few celebrity spokespersons that you would recognize from television were onstage sharing their knowledge. Since I'd been in the beauty industry for years, I thought of many of these people as friends, but as I said hello to them I noticed that my daughter saw them as something else: super-successful or even famous.

That night when we were at the hotel having dinner—it was our tradition to order noodles from Xian Famous Foods in the West Village and bring them back to our room—we had a conversation about what she wanted to do with her life, and she couldn't stop talking about all of the people I'd introduced her to that day. That's when it struck me that there were three things that each of my successful friends had in common, and it didn't matter if they'd grown up rich or poor, what race they were, where they were born, if they were male or female, gay or straight. I mentioned this to Emma, who was intrigued. Then I remembered that I had a presentation on my iPad called "19 Ideas for Success" that I had shared for years with new stylists as well as beauty school and high school students, yet I had never shared it with her. I asked if she'd be interested in hearing some of the wisdom I'd acquired over the years. To my delight she said yes, and just like that this book was born.

My wife Leah and I have another daughter named Claire, who is three years younger than her sister, and while I can't tell you how Emma's or Claire's lives will turn out, I can share two quick stories with you. Emma will be entering her senior year in high school so she is having those "I don't know what I want to do when I get older" and "I don't know where I want to go to college" moments. Recently I told her that there are people in college right now who are studying photography because they want to photograph rock bands, but she has already done that because she used one of the tools I'll share in this book: "Never Be a Consideration, Always Be a Yes or No." So while other people are waiting for their big break, Emma has already had hers because she had the courage to contact bands like Missio, Airways and Iron Tom and ask if she could photograph them.

One afternoon Claire, who has always walked like she was going somewhere and has an attitude that will change the world someday, told my wife and me that Emma was going to a job fair at a local ski resort and that she had decided to go, too. Our first question was, "Do they even hire 14-year-olds?" Her answer: "Yes." So how could she be so sure? She called and asked. I turned to Leah and said, "We don't have to worry about her; she is always going to know how to make a job for herself."

As Artistic Director for a few of the top beauty brands in the world, including some Fortune 500 companies, I have been fortunate enough to teach in more than 15 countries on five continents. The advice I'll share in this book, the same advice I shared with Emma in that hotel room in New York City, is truly universal. I have collected these ideas from people I've met in Africa, Asia, Australia, New Zealand, Europe and North America.

I've divided the book into three parts. In the first, which focuses on success, I'll share the three things that all of my successful friends have in common. In the second, which focuses on money, I'll share the three things that all of my friends who are financially secure have in common. In the third, I'll share the 19 ideas I've collected over the years from very successful people who have kept me from getting in my own way as I've moved through my life. So, let's begin.

SECTION ONE
THREE KEYS TO SUCCESS

Recently my wife and I were watching the Netflix docu-series *Abstract*, which is written and directed by my brother-in-law, Morgan Neville, who also happened to win an Oscar for *20 Feet from Stardom*, the documentary he directed about backup singers who live in a world that lies just beyond the spotlight. *Abstract* tells the stories of innovative, creative people, like Tinker Haven Hatfield, Jr., 66, who has designed numerous athletic shoes for Nike, from the Air Jordan 3 through the Air Jordan 15; Platon, 50, a British photographer who has taken portraits of many presidents and other world figures; and Bjarke Ingels, 43, a Danish architect known for his buildings that defy convention, while incorporating sustainable design principles.

The series got me thinking about what it means to excel in a particular field, to make your mark in the world, and it reinforced something I'd already told Emma, namely that successful people have three things in common. Like I realized when talking to Emma in that hotel room in New York City, it doesn't matter where they grew up, if they're an entrepreneur or a corporate leader, if they're male or female, gay or straight. None of that matters, but there are three things that successful people have in common.

#1 THE FIVE PEOPLE THEY HANG OUT WITH THE MOST ARE BETTER THAN THEM

One thing I've noticed about my successful friends is that they tend to hang out with people who are better than them at whatever it is they're doing. Want to become a better golfer? Play golf with people who are better than you are. They'll challenge you to become a better golfer.

When I started coloring hair in 1987, women began to think about hair color as a fashion statement, not just something they had to do to cover gray or fulfill their blonde ambitions. At the time all of the big names in the beauty industry were haircutters, but I was working at the top salons in New York City and coloring hair for some of the top hair color brands on the market. Supermodels were making a name for themselves, and hair color was a big deal. Because I was only 22, it's safe to say that everyone I worked with was better than I was, and what a gift that turned out to be. When I became Color Director at a prestigious salon in Manhattan, I put together a team of people who were far more talented and experienced than I was. That meant that I had to show up every day and work my butt off just to keep up with them, and it kept me on top of my game.

Some of the successful people I've met over the years have become friends, and I've learned a lot from them. A well-known motivational speaker and author told me that he only flies first-class, an upgrade he pays for out of his own pocket. Now I love first-class as much as the next guy, but I always flew coach, having bought into the conventional wisdom that there were better things I could do with the money I saved. When I asked him why he only flew first-class, he looked at me and said, "All of my clients are sitting in first-class." That was my *aha* moment. Paying for first-class allowed him to spend his time networking with people who could actually further his career, which is a lot more productive than playing solitaire on your iPhone in coach.

One of my closest friends taught me a similar lesson recently when we were discussing our vacation plans and he told me that he and his family would be staying at The Four Seasons when they went to Hawaii on their vacation. Now this is a guy who grew up so poor that even though he excelled at certain sports, he wasn't able to participate because his family couldn't afford the equipment. I couldn't help but laugh when this same guy told me that he was going to stay at The Four Seasons. Still laughing, I asked him why he was going to The Four Seasons in Hawaii. You know what he told me? "You won't believe who you meet at the pool." You know what? He was right. He not only had a great vacation, but he also he came back from that trip to Kona with some great business contacts.

Here's another case in point: When my daughter and I were discussing which colleges she should apply to, I asked her if she knew why it was important to go to a good school. When she said, "To get a good education," I shook my head. The reason for going to a good college, I told her, was because she would be surrounded by like-minded, successful people, who could be a catalyst for her own success one day. The bottom line: The reason for going to a prestigious college or working with a great team of people is that the people around you will help you, teach you, hold you accountable and let you grow.

It's not by accident that I refer to good colleges and great teams. I have not completed my own four-year degree. Even though I had achieved Phi Beta Kappa status, I stopped taking classes before graduating because I was on the road so much for Clairol and wasn't able to attend classes regularly. If only online education had been available in 1987, I would have finished my degree. Still, many successful people from Apple founder Steve Jobs on down never graduated from college, but the lessons they learned and the people they met in an academic environment were invaluable.

So who are the five people in your life you spend the most time with, both at work and outside of work. Are they the right people? Is it time to reevaluate your choices? I'm reminded of one of the NFL's greats, New England Patriot Aaron Hernandez, whose life took a tragic turn when he lost his father due to a medical error. During a very short period of time right after his father's death, the friends he made were not good people. Later in life when struggles occurred, instead of looking for support from his teammates, like Tom Brady, he surrounded himself with a crew of gangsters, hitting the clubs and missing workout sessions with a rehab trainer. Ultimately, his career came to an abrupt end when he was arrested for the murder of one his friends. Sadly, Hernandez took his own life while in prison.

The point is, the people you hang out with can determine your future. So if you're frustrated because you haven't achieved the results in life you were looking for, look around. Are you the best member on your team? In other words, have you gone as far as you can with the team you're on? Imagine where Justin Timberlake would be now if he never left NSYNC and went out on his own.

Let's say you're thinking that you would like to pursue a career in music like Justin did. To make that dream a reality, you need to make a decision about where you want to live. Ambitious, talented people move to big cities like New York, Los Angeles, London or Paris all the time because they're the center of art, culture, entertainment and creativity. Want to be a country music star? Then moving to Nashville makes sense because that's where you'll meet the right people to further your career. Today you can be discovered on YouTube, but true success comes from surrounding yourself with the right people.

I remember hopping into a cab when I was in Chicago for business and asking the driver to take me to the Convention Center where I was going to be a speaker. As we pulled away from the curb, he asked if I was successful. I told him that I was, and he asked if I was a stockbroker. When I explained that I was a hairdresser, he told me that he wanted to be a stockbroker. I asked him if he hung out with stockbrokers, and he said, "No, I hang out with cab drivers." My first thought was that he would continue driving a cab instead of working on Wall Street.

In the movie, *The Wolf of Wall Street*, Donnie Azoff (Jonah Hill) took an entry-level job with Jordan Belfort (Leonardo DiCaprio) at a Wall Street brokerage firm after Belfort showed him his pay stub. While still in his 20s, Belfort found his own firm and hired a band of brokers, all of whom became enormously successful because they honed their craft by studying the master. It's why people who move to Hollywood to break into the movie industry take low-paying jobs in the mailroom just to be around the people they want to become someday.

So to recap, here's the first thing that all of my successful friends have in common: The people they spend the most time with, outside of immediate family, are more successful than them. Period. End of story.

#2 THEY TRAVEL

"The world is like a book, and those who do not travel read only one page."—
Saint Augustine

All of my successful friends travel, and it's made all the difference in their lives.

I went to England to teach hair color at the age of 23 and then to Germany at 24, which jump-started my career at home. Traveling to Africa in my mid-30s changed my life. I was born in New York but had been to California where our family rented a car and drove to Mexico. I had also spent a week in Jamaica at an all-inclusive resort, but none of those trips had exposed me to anything that was authentic. As a young man working in Manhattan, I saw no reason to leave the city, which was the center of fashion and culture. I went to Cleveland, Ohio, for an event called the "International Look" where two guest artists—one from England and one from Germany—were brought in to share the latest trends with hairdressers from the Midwest. I was one of two colorists who were invited to color the models' hair, and I was paired with the English artist.

Right away I noticed that the German hairdresser seemed to be all alone so I invited him to join me and the English artist for dinner. Every night we walked across the street to eat at the same Mexican restaurant because we didn't have a car and it was snowing hard. After the event wrapped up, both of the guest artists invited me to teach at their salon groups. One year later I went to England for nine days, culminating in an offer to be the Technical/Color Director at a very prestigious salon group there. I declined their offer since New York City was the center of fashion and culture at the time, but saying no allowed me to do something I now call "Doing the Jimi Hendrix," something only travel offers.

An African-American rock guitarist, singer and songwriter, Hendrix went to England in the 1960s where his reception was far different than it was back home. Bands like the Beatles and The Rolling Stones were fascinated with black musicians from America like Chuck Berry, Muddy Waters, Howlin' Wolf and B.B. King, and they welcomed Hendrix into the fold. By the time he returned to the United States with three Top Ten hits in the UK, he had changed the sound of music forever.

I had a similar experience. Being a hairdresser from New York City gave me a certain cachet that made me marketable in Great Britain, and I was invited to teach there at age 23. When I came home, I was a known commodity who had already proven myself, and I was sought out by the legendary hairdresser John Sahag, who asked

me to work on models for a workshop he held at his salon in
Manhattan.

Being a New York City hair colorist has enabled me to "Jimi
Hendrix" myself all over the world, working in more than 15
countries on five continents. What's more, every time I come back
from one of those trips new opportunities present themselves. If
you go the right places at the right time it's money in the bank. And
if you know your metrics—the cost vs. the income opportunity—
this kind of travel can be very profitable.

Before I got married, I planned all of my vacations to coincide with
places where I got paid to teach or speak. Every time I came home,
my clients and co-workers would be impressed with where I'd been
and what I had done there.

At the time I was working for the largest U.S.-based hair color
company in the world, and one afternoon I got a call from the
president of the company, who had heard that I was teaching in
Germany. Imagine my surprise when he told me that he needed my
help. Apparently he was having trouble getting his products into
salons in Germany and asked if I could help. I did and got a
promotion. Then, when I was just 26, a German-based hair color
company asked me to become their National Technical Training
Manager for the U.S. and Canada. This is how travel changed my
career trajectory.

Travel has also changed me personally. As a Native Yorker, my "normal" was towering buildings, crowds of people in the streets, automobiles stalled in traffic and honking their horns, subways hurtling to the five boroughs, and people arriving in the city from all over the world. What visiting Africa taught me was that those things were normal for me but not necessarily for everyone else. The truth is, for millions of years, normal meant living with no central heating, no AC, no running water, no security, no closets full of clothes, no Internet, and all while living under the constant threat of imminent danger. When I went to Africa in 2003, I stayed in Johannesburg, a major city not unlike New York. Still, for a vast majority of people living in remote areas, life hadn't changed much for them. Their "normal" might not include running water or electricity.

As I returned to New York City from that trip and emerged from the subway to see the Empire State Building, I realized that "my normal" was not "normal" at all. The more I travel, the more I appreciate the normals I have or occasionally realize that some of what I call normal no longer serves any purpose.

What I can tell you from personal experience is that travel makes a difference. It broadens your horizons and your outlook on life. You become a better person by traveling, and when you travel with a purpose it can fast-track your career.

#3 THEY CREATE THEIR JOBS/SUCCESS

The third thing that all of my successful friends have in common is that they create their own success. They don't just get jobs; they create new ways of thinking about their jobs and businesses. It doesn't matter if they inherited the family business, worked their way up the corporate ladder or started their own companies, all of my successful friends put their own spin on what they do.

Steve Jobs is a good example. When he returned to Apple for the second time, he didn't create a better computer; he changed the way we interact with technology. The iPod changed the way we hear music. iTunes changed the way we buy music. The iPhone changed the way we communicate.

Not long ago I watched *Sky Ladder*, a great documentary on the Chinese artist Cai Guo-Qiang, who paints with gunpowder and uses fireworks to create works of art both on canvas and in the sky. It was his travels to Japan as a young man that helped him learn to control his creative medium. As the Director of Visual and Special Effects for the 2008 Summer Olympics in Beijing, he is responsible for the pyrotechnics spectacle silhouetting the "Bird's Nest" during the opening ceremony. There is a scene in *Sky Ladder* where Steven

Spielberg is examining one of Guo-Qiang's canvases—a huge work of art with portraits, mountains and other images burnt into the canvas. After a moment, Spielberg asks the artist how many explosions it took to create that canvas. After a pause, the translator replies, "One." Suffice it to say that Spielberg was visibly blown away by the artist's control and could only mutter, "one" in amazement. Like all the successful people I've known, Guo-Qiang put his own spin on his craft and made it his own. From brands like McDonald's and Starbucks to entrepreneurs like Steve Jobs and Virgin Group founder Sir Richard Branson, visionaries have always changed the way we think and how we live.

My wife Leah and I have been together for a long time. We met when she was just 18 years old and I was 24 and started dating a few months later. We've been together ever since, which is now more than half our lives. During out time together, Leah graduated from the Fashion Institute of Technology with two degrees and worked her way up through the display department at Nordstrom to become Manager/Head of Display for the entire store by the time she was 26. Then when she was 28, she had our first daughter and made a decision to be a stay-at-home mom.

Now here's where the story gets interesting. For the next 16 years Leah raised our daughters while keeping track of and submitting my travel expenses and then handling payroll, HR and accounting for two salons we opened in Pennsylvania. By the time the girls were older and she started looking for a fulltime job, Leah found that no one wanted to hire her. Even with her two degrees and her years of experience working behind the scenes at our salons, she could not get a decent job that utilized her skills. Applying for a position as a receptionist at an assisted living facility, she was told that she was unqualified because she didn't have enough experience as a receptionist. Disheartened, she took a job at a local warehouse making just above minimum wage.

"I never thought I'd end up working in a warehouse," she told our youngest daughter, who found her crying one day and asked what was wrong. Still, Leah knew she had to work and took the warehouse job.

Then, out of the blue, she got a call from Nordstrom. The chain was opening a new location about 45 minutes away from where we lived. Leah had applied for a position online before she took the job in the warehouse, but it had taken this long for them to schedule an interview. Ultimately Leah was offered a position as Assistant Manager but not in her field since the store did not have a display department. After we talked it over, Leah decided not to accept the offer because the job at the warehouse was closer to home and did not require work on weekends, nights or holidays.

Still, having been married to someone who has owned his own businesses since before we were married, Leah thinks like an entrepreneur and began making suggestions at work that maximized surface space and efficiency. She also created team-building exercises for her team, started a Warehouse Olympics, and worked with engineers to develop her idea for connecting racks together. Let's just say that she has not run out of ideas. Now she loves her job and loves her life. One year after our daughter found her crying about settling for a job in a warehouse, Leah was promoted twice, first to Specialist and then to Supervisor. The point is, my wife not only created jobs, but she also made a life she loves that allows her to drop the girls off at school every morning and offers paid holidays plus travel to cities like San Francisco and Dallas.

The designer Tom Ford's story is surprisingly similar. When Gucci was struggling to pay staff and was laying people off, Ford found himself with the opportunity to design the things he wanted to because there was no one else left and he didn't even know if he was going to be paid or not. Madonna loved his designs. So did fashionistas in Hollywood and New York City. Ford not only became the head of design at Gucci but went on to create his own line of clothing and perfumes for men and women. He even directed the Academy Award-nominated films, *A Single Man* and *Nocturnal Animals*. In other words, Tom Ford has always made his own jobs.

Oprah Winfrey struggled with abuse her entire young life. The only future her grandmother could imagine for her was a job working for a good family. But Oprah defied the odds and followed her own path, parlaying her first job as the youngest person to co-anchor the news at WTVF, a CBS-affiliated television station in Nashville, into an empire that includes every form of media. Oprah not only became a household name, but she also became the first female African-American billionaire.

I have asked for every job I ever had except for one. I wrote blogs for several trade magazines because I called the editors and simply asked if I could. John Lennon famously said that life is what happens while you're making other plans, but I disagree. Life is what you make of it, and creating the job you want is the best way I know to create a life worth living.

SECTION II
THREE KEYS TO FINANCIAL SUCCESS

People have often said of hairdressers, "They're either wearing their money or driving it." Let's face it, we've all indulged in a little retail therapy from time to time, but it's not exactly a long-term strategy for achieving financial security or what I like to call financial means, which is simply having enough money to cover basic living expenses like food and shelter without daily financial worry. Let's say your car needs an unexpected repair. Would you have enough money in savings to cover the cost without going into debt? Or let's say you wanted to take the family on a vacation. Do you earn enough money to comfortably put something aside each month in order to make those plans a reality? Most likely you do if you're bringing in between $50,000 to $75,000 a year. In cities like New York or Los Angeles, you'll need to earn as much as $85,000 to $150,000 per capita.

Now if you think that making significantly more money will buy you happiness, you're wrong. There's a tipping point above which money will not buy happiness and may also lead to depression, self-injury or even suicide. We've seen this with celebrities who seemed to have it all but over-dose on drugs or take their own lives. American rapper Biggie Smalls—The Notorious B.I.G.—put it this way: "More money, more problems." Think about people who have multiple houses, cars and private jets, yet they're still not happy.

Brickman and Campbell coined the term "hedonic adaptation" in their 1971 essay, *"Hedonic Relativism and Planning the Good Society."* During the late 1990s, Michael Eysenck, a British psychologist, modified the concept, calling it the "hedonic treadmill theory," but this notion that happiness has a set point can be traced all the way back to St. Augustine. "A true saying it is, Desire hath no rest, is infinite in itself, endless, and as one calls it, a perpetual rack, or horse-mill."

For most of us, making enough money for food, clothing, a car, a house, an education or a vacation is a goal that offers hope for a better future. On the other hand, some people who get everything they ever hoped for find that it's not enough or, in the worst case, that they're not enough.

The three keys to financial success that I will share here I've learned from observing friends who are financially secure, i.e. have enough money to live comfortably.

#4 THEY UNDERSTAND THAT THERE ARE ONLY 100 PENNIES IN EVERY DOLLAR

When I opened my first brick-and-mortar business at 28, I wanted to make sure I did things right. That meant seeking out people I knew in the industry who could teach me the things I didn't know. I have one very good friend, who is a genius when it comes to business. I asked him to tell me what the best piece of advice he ever got was, just one thing that he never forgot. Here's what he said: "There are only 100 pennies in every dollar." If you could have seen the thought bubble over my head, the words inside would have read, "Thanks a blanking lot." Since I'd asked him for one piece of advice, I couldn't ask a follow-up question, and for a few months I didn't understand how profound his answer was. As I matured as a salon owner, I grasped the significance of that piece of advice he gave me. If there are only 100 pennies in every dollar, there are 100 percentage points in 100 percent. The challenge for me was to save a few percentage points or even ¼ of a percentage point, which over time would add up to big money. So I started to order my sundry items from a large distributor halfway across the country instead of my local supplier in order to save between 20 to 30 percent on every order. Admittedly orders took longer and I needed to plan ahead and order larger quantities each time, but I knew that eventually we'd use these items and that I was saving 25 percent, which was like getting my fifth order for free.

The truth is, most people purchase things using each of those 100 pennies in a dollar. If they use a credit card to make those purchases, they may also be paying interest, which is pointless, like trying to squeeze 115 or 128 pennies out of a dollar that only has 100. It's also a mistake not waiting for sales or not using coupons and sites like E-Bates to save money. Big-box stores also offer coupons good for 20% off, some of which are available on your smart phone. Not taking advantage of these deals is like throwing pennies away. The key is to make ever penny count and make money by watching pennies and percentages.

Here are some ways I make every penny count and even make a few more from time to time:

Get a credit card

I have two: one for business and one for personal use. The one I use for business has a small yearly fee, earns points and offers percentages back for business purchases that can be converted into debit cards, travel or merchandise my business can use. My grandfather taught me to buy everything with a credit card. The only caveat was that I had to wait until I had enough money in savings to pay those purchases off within 30 days and not incur interest. The advantages of this strategy, he explained, were two-fold. First, if I held on to my money in an interest-bearing account,

I'd make money while waiting for the credit card bill to arrive. The second advantage was that having a credit card I paid off each month was a good way to build credit. This was way before things like platinum cards existed or we were able to earn points by using our credit cards, but by following my grandfather's advice I was able to purchase a three-bedroom townhome when I was only 26 years old. The bottom line is that as long as you have money in your pocket or your bank account, use credit and earn some points with that money.

What can you do with pre-tax dollars?
The wonderful thing about S-Corps and LLC's is that they let you use pre-tax dollars to build your business. Most people don't understand how important this is. For example, someone making a moderate income brings home about 72 of those 100 pennies in every dollar after taxes. A business, on the other hand, is not taxed on the profit it makes until it pays for operating expenses. That means that only the pennies left after all the bills are paid are taxed. See the difference? The average person pays their expenses with the 72 pennies that were left after taxes, while a business owner has all 100 pennies to work with. This is why a company car, company planes and even apartments are affordable for so many businesses, while they're unattainable for so many individuals. Imagine if everything you needed to do you could do with 28 more pennies in every dollar.

That's where a 401k or an IRA comes into play for anyone who is earning an income and for those lucky individuals who work for the companies that still match their contributions. Let's say your company matches even $50. That's $50 you didn't have before. What's more, many of these programs use pre-tax dollars, which means that 100 pennies are going in—not 100 pennies that were taxed and became 72 pennies but a full 100 pennies. Even better, the pre-tax contribution lowers your taxable income, which may put you in a lower tax bracket. So instead of the government taxing you for all the money you made, you can subtract the money you saved by investing in a 401k or IRA, up to the maximum amount, and pay taxes on that money later when you might be retired or making less money, reducing the amount of taxes you'll owe.

The bottom line is that whether you're an individual with a 401k or IRA or a business or LLC, pre-tax dollars give you a lot more pennies to purchase things you need or to build a nest-egg. Think about this: A credit card processing company charges a minimum of 2.7 percent every time a customer swipes their card, and even that seemingly miniscule amount adds up to big bucks. So think about how much money your 28 pennies out of every 100 can add up to. Check with your accountant and current tax laws to see what's allowable.

Specials and Bulk

There are good and bad times to buy everything, and during an emergency is definitely not the best time. So ask yourself what you *have* to buy, what you *need* to buy and what you *want* to buy.

A company car is a good example. If you want to be a limo driver or operate a snowplowing business, the right car or truck would be something you *have* to buy unless you already own one of these vehicles. The right vehicle would be a start-up expense, and you might need after-tax pennies from another source of income to get going. Many people have mortgaged their houses or used credit cards to start their first business, essentially using money that had already been taxed or incurring interest charges that made the money even more expensive. The fact is, the things you have to buy when you're starting a business are expensive.

Realtors or people who own a cleaning business often require a company vehicle, but if they can use their personal vehicle to get the business going, they buy some time in which to save enough pre-tax dollars to buy a second vehicle for company use. But what about the things people want to buy, like a beautiful new car every three years? A Realtor or limo drive might be able to afford a car that's a little bit better because it's the car the business needs. In this case money should not be a challenge because they are fulfilling a want, not a need, and have the time to shop for the best deal.

Taking advantage of specials and deals depends on whether or not you *have* to buy something right away. If that's the case, buy it but save the most pennies by comparison shopping. Ask friends for recommendations or search for the best deal online. For the things you *need* to buy, do your research. For example, look into savings when buying in bulk. For things you *want* to buy, set hard goals and use these as rewards for your hard work, making sure there are more than enough pennies left after you get what you wanted. If you are successful and want to purchase the kinds of high-end or top-shelf items that say something about your brand, it's probably a safe investment and may actually help to grow your business.

Here is my rule: Have to buy, use the money you have; need to buy, wait until you have the money to buy it; want to buy, wait until it's on special.

#5 THEY UNDERSTAND THE DIFFERENCE BETWEEN AN EXPENSE AND AN INVESTMENT, INCLUDING THE DIFFERENCE BETWEEN GOOD DEBT AND BAD DEBT

The difference between an expense and an investment may depend upon the timing or the company. Like I mentioned earlier, one of my friends, who is a consultant, only flies first class and pays for it himself because "all of my clients are sitting in first class." That means his first-class tickets are a legitimate business expense that can be written off since traveling that way has become a marketing strategy that has paid off by attracting new clients.

As a speaker with his own business who travels globally, he has earned the right to be sitting up front in first class. It makes sense for his business because a high-paid speaker like him has very few of the traditional operating expenses such as a large payroll, janitorial services and so on, freeing up money that can be used for a first-class ticket that might generate new business. Of course, when he was just starting out in business, he sat in the back of the bus so to speak like everyone else. At that point in his career, a first-class ticket would have been more of an expense than an investment. Why? Because he had not earned the right to be sitting in first class yet. Sure, he was ambitious and hungry, but at that point he had not done enough to impress a CEO, VP or anyone else in a position of importance at a large company. He could talk the talk, but successful people know who is walking the walk, and he hadn't walked the walk yet.

I have a very simple metric when it comes to investing in my business. I want $10 back for every $1 that I put in. I also want people who hire me to make $10 for every $1 they invest in working with me. Honestly, if people aren't thinking this way then I'm not an investment and they will not be able to afford to work with me again. Hopefully the money you spent on this book has already given you a 10 to 1 return on your investment.

Taking out a mortgage or paying rent on a prime business location is an investment, whereas an $800 monthly payment on a student loan might just be a life-long expense. The problem with $1 worth of debt that is an expense and not an investment is that it costs way more than $1 to pay it off after taxes, interest, expenses and so on. And $1 worth of good debt that is an investment can save you as much as 28% just by using pre-tax dollars for business expenses. When you begin making capital investments into things that make your business more efficient, effective and visible for growth, even more pennies become available to build that business you always wanted.

Good debt is owning the building that houses your business or even owning the equipment or other things you need to operate a business so you don't have to rent anything. When you pay rent on the space you use for business, you are making someone else rich. When you have a mortgage on the space you use for business, you own a little bit more of that space with every payment you make. Essentially you're paying rent to yourself and saving more of the pennies in each dollar with every payment you make.

Bad debt can be an over-the-top remodel that actually distracts from the business. Expansion of business offerings can also become bad debt. A case in point: A well-known coffee chain made an investment in its business by diversifying its food offerings and invested in more automated machines rather than the traditional machines their baristas were known for using. When the place started to smell more like food than coffee, their investment ended up becoming a huge expense. Not only did they lose a lot of business, but they also had to retrofit all their stores and even shut down all the stores for part of one day to retrain all of their employees. Good debt makes you money, while bad debt always costs more money.

#6 THEY UNDERSTAND YOU CAN'T LIVE ON TOMORROW, BUT YOU CAN BUILD ON TODAY

Too many people have plans for making money tomorrow, maybe even "hitting it big" or winning the lottery, and they live their lives at the edge of financial ruin while waiting for that to happen. Then there are people who surprise us, like Ronald Reed, who was a janitor his whole life, yet left $6 million to a local library and hospital when he died. Former school teacher Margaret Southern left $8.4 million to a local community foundation that benefited children and animals. Neither of those people ever earned a lot of money in their lifetimes, but they knew that putting even a little bit away every week was a better strategy for achieving financial independence than hoping to win the lottery.

I have been lucky. I started saving when I was young. With my father's help I began investing in the stock market when I was just 14 years old, and I purchased my first house at 26 even though I had never made more than $30,000 a year. Actually, the fact that I did not earn a lot of money made it possible to get a reduced rate for people with low incomes. I have always had a mortgage, have never accumulated a penny of credit card debt and have made the maximum contribution allowed by law to my 401k every year. Now at 51 years old and with a wife and two children, I can you tell you unequivocally that this strategy has worked for me.

Ways to Feather Your Nest

Pre-Tax Dollars

Everything you can do pre-tax, do it, from a 401K to an IRA. If you can pay for your health care with pre-tax dollars, do it. Take any pre-tax deductions the law permits. Right there you are using 100 pennies, building on today and taking care of tomorrow and what could happen.

Play Games

Our oldest daughter decided to save all of the $5 bills she got for one year and ended up with a very nice nest egg for a 15-year-old. I have had friends who relied on tips to supplement their income and saved every $20 bill they got. Others saved everything up to $100 and spent the rest. So if they made $134 in tips, they would spend $34 and save $100. When I worked for other people and got a raise, I always lived on the amount I made before the raise and saved the rest automatically with direct deposit. I even save my change in an old glass wine jug, which adds up and allows me to do some fun things.

Extra Payments/Full Payments

The metrics of what one extra mortgage payment applied to the principle per year is exponential in its impact. A single 13th payment can lower a 30-year mortgage to 26 years, a 15- year mortgage to just less than 12 years. One of my favorites is saving the 2% many quarterly bills offer if you pay in full for the year. What's amazing is how fast that 2% turns into big money when many times I am also paying those bills on my credit card, which is earning me another 2% and building for a bright future. Think about it this way: 2% x 10 years is 20% savings x 2 if I pay with my credit card and get points or cash back.

The thing about money is that people either choose to understand how money works or they just think it is something you spend. I will talk more about this later in the book. There are many well-documented examples of Lottery winners who won more money than they ever needed and didn't understand how money works so they lost all of their millions in just a few years.

The secret to accumulating money is to have your money making money for you and having the money in savings for things you need before you spend your money on things you want. I have a lot of friends who make a million dollars and spend a million and one. The truth is, it's not how much you make, it's how much you keep and use to make more money.

SECTION THREE
19 THINGS I LEARNED ALONG THE WAY

#7 EXPERIENCE IS THE ABILITY TO RECOGNIZE A MISTAKE WHEN I AM ABOUT TO MAKE IT AGAIN

Sometimes wisdom or inspiration comes from the most unlikely places, and I have learned to be ready to recognize it. One such place was on a packet of sugar. Before we were married, my wife and I used to have breakfast—eggs and a pile of bacon—every Sunday morning at a classic greasy spoon that served amazing coffee. It was just one of those things that we loved to do. As I was pouring sugar in my coffee on one of those lazy Sunday mornings, I noticed a quote on the side of the packet of sugar. It reminded me of those messages we get in fortune cookies at Chinese restaurants. The message on my "Fortune Sugar Packet" struck me as profound at the time: "Experience is the ability to recognize a mistake when I am about to make it again."

At this point in my life I was hanging out only with people who were better than me. In fact, many of them were plainly out of my league. Still, they liked me and saw that I could learn and eventually keep up. So even though I was young when this message came into my life, it made instant sense to me. Over the years I've thought about how these words apply to everything from my friendships to the way I do business. Let me explain.

Friendship

I have very few close friends, as do my wife and both of our children. My mother once described friendship to me this way: Unlike people you meet because of circumstances like where you live or work or worship, friends are people in whom you invest time and energy over the long haul. Think about your neighbors who moved away or people you worked with who left to pursue other opportunities. How often did you stay in touch with them? I have a lot of "friends" like that, people I once cared for very much, but the reality is that I have only a few close friends, people who have been in my life for a very long time.

Sometimes we make mistakes when it comes to the friends we choose. I've experienced the normal run-of-the-mill betrayals, but I've also lost an enormous amount of money in a business deal gone bad with a "friend." One "friend" downloaded my entire database of clients and took that information to another salon while I was on an extended business trip before giving two-weeks notice.

Many people are fooled by my surname, which leads people to assume that I am Irish. The truth is, I am half-Italian and spent a lot of time with my Italian grandparents growing up. Like many families of Italian descent, my family took great pride in their heritage. My grandmother's family was from Naples, while my grandfather's family came from Sicily. Let's just say that we had many lively discussions over Sunday dinners at their house. When my Sicilian grandfather used to ask us who we were, we'd get a dollar if we answered, "Italian and Irish." To answer, "Irish and Italian" was to go home empty-handed.

There are two expressions I apply to my friendships. One is, "Fool me once, shame on you. Fool me twice, shame on me." The other is, "Sicilian dead." Most of you are probably familiar with the first expression but less familiar with the second one. Let me explain. I try to give a friend the benefit of the doubt, at least at first, but if I find out that something they did was done deliberately to hurt me or my family, they are "Sicilian dead" to me, which means that they might as well not exist. I don't look for them, search for them or acknowledge them in any way. I do not walk away from our friendship in anger, but if I passed them on the street, it would be no more impactful than passing a billboard on the highway. Cue the soundtrack to *The Godfather*. The Corleones knew a little something about the concept of someone being "Sicilian dead" to them.

Business

To keep from making the same mistakes in business again and again, I have reached out to people I trust so I can learn from their experiences. I am reminded of another expression about how some people learn from their mistakes, while smart people learn from the mistakes others have made. Experience is invaluable when things don't go as well as expected.

Both experienced and inexperienced people may realize a great outcome from a similar set of circumstances. The difference is that an inexperienced person may not even understand what is happening when faced with an unexpected outcome, while an experienced individual not only knows what's going on but also how to fix it because it probably happened to them before.

For me, much of life is not about learning how to do something right; it's how to keep things from going wrong. When my daughters were young, they asked me how to ride a bicycle. I told them that the key was to figure out how not to fall off because I had learned from experience that there are actually a lot of ways to *ride* a bike.

#8 I'M NOT THAT SPECIAL

My flight home from a business trip had just landed at our regional airport when my phone began to ring. When I picked up, my wife cried dramatically, "Why does this always happen to me?"

My first instinct was to ask about our girls, and she assured me that they were fine. My wife, however, was not. She explained that she had hit a car while trying to find a vacant spot in the airport parking lot. After she calmed down, I told her to go back to the car she hit and put a note on the windshield that included her name, phone number and the name of our insurance carrier.

"By the way," I told her, "you're not that special."

"What does that mean?" she asked.

"You started this conversation by asking why this always happens to you, but the fact is that it doesn't," I explained. "You're not so special that you hit a car every day. That's why it's called an accident. And what lesson do we want to teach our girls, who are sitting in the backseat?"

About a month later, Leah told me that she had never heard from the person whose car she hit. We both thought that was strange, but when he finally reached out, he told Leah that he hadn't even noticed that she hit his car until the next morning when he saw the note on his windshield. He apologized for taking so long to get back to her, but he had gone to the trouble of getting a few estimates when the first one was, in his opinion, too high. Then he said something that really surprised us. His wife was being treated for cancer, and the fact that Leah was honest enough to leave a note claiming responsibility for the accident and offering to pay for the damage was the best thing that had happened to him in months.

I was glad that Leah had set a good example for our girls by doing the right thing, but it also made me wonder about how often we do something that seems insignificant to us but means so much to someone else.

"I'm not that special" doesn't mean that no one is special. It just means that we are all special. No one is so special that they get hit by all the raindrops when it's raining, but none of us is so special that we don't get hit by any of the raindrops when it's raining either. What makes us special is what we do when we get hit with those raindrops. Are we complaining that we are wet? Or are we singing in the rain?

Life is not extraordinary because someone is special. People are special because they create an extraordinary life.

#9 NEVER BE A CONSIDERATION, ALWAYS BE A YES OR NO

Almost everything I have done in life is because I looked around, saw what people were doing or weren't doing and told someone what I wanted to do for them. Sometimes the first answer was "no," which isn't necessarily a bad thing.

Let's say you wanted to style the hair or photograph a cover for a top fashion magazine. Now let's imagine that you had the opportunity to meet the editor in chief of that magazine and ask her for that opportunity. The chances of her saying "yes" to your request are probably slim to none, but that doesn't mean the end of the road for you. After one of my closest friends cut a very well-known actress's hair short, she was so impressed that she had him do her hair for everything from awards shows to magazine covers to a global ad campaign. Still, when it came to him doing her hair for the cover of *Vogue*, the answer was "no."

As it turns out, *Vogue* has a handful of hairdressers who are approved to do covers for the magazine, and while they acknowledged that my friend is extremely talented, he just isn't on that list yet. He was very cool about the whole thing, said that he understood and hoped that one day his prospects might change.

I use this story to make a point, which is that the moment you get a "no" from someone, you have gone from being a non-entity to being a "no." Just getting their attention allows you to ask what you'd have to do to earn the opportunity to be part of the team that creates their cover looks. You have graduated from not even being a consideration to being on their radar. Now the door is open a crack, not just slammed in your face.

Knowing what path to take in life is a complex process. Sometimes we invest large sums of money in things or take jobs because we think we need to in order to be successful, but often a "no" helps us get a better understanding of where we should invest our time and energy.

The secret is to let people know what you want to do, but you'd better be prepared to knock it out of the park if they say "yes" or you may not get asked again. If you get a "no," ask what you can do to be ready for an opportunity when it presents itself in the future. It's fine to have plans and dreams, but also be prepared to answer the door when opportunity knocks.

Many, many, many times in my life I have had people tell me about their goals and dreams, like traveling to exotic places for work, working backstage at premiere fashion and celebrity events, or even working directly with celebrities. What frustrates me is how unprepared many of them are. Some admit that they aren't morning people, which is a red flag since these kinds of opportunities require long hours. Others may not have a credit card because of bad debt, while many of them don't have a passport, which they'd need if the opportunity to travel internationally suddenly presented itself.

The truth is, no one should ever feel like they don't deserve a chance to take advantage of opportunities, but it's important to start doing what you can today so that you are prepared when the answer is "yes." Ask yourself if you have people in your personal life who support you. Do you have the financial means to travel? Do you have a flexible work schedule that permits you to pick up and take off for extended periods of time?

I've had multiple opportunities—from being an artistic director making a six-figure salary to writing a blog to doing the shows I dreamed of—all because I asked for them. I had a friend who asked me why the company I worked for always let me travel with the same lead person even though everyone else used local people as leads for their events. The answer, of course, was because I asked.

#10 CREATE AN EXPERIENCE

Many times the difference between good and great is the experience, but that wasn't always the case. Years ago most of us thought that a product that worked as expected was great, while the one that frequently underperformed was good. Today's savvy consumers can research their options—and they have plenty of them—in order to avoid buying junk. So what do people buy?

When it comes to the world of personal computers, Apple was a game changer. Before Steve Jobs decided that people would pay more for good design, everyone settled for bland, beige PCs that were relatively inexpensive. The iMac, which came in a beautiful shade of teal blue, was a self-contained unit that was easy to use. Sure, it was more expensive than a PC, but people loved it. In fact, Apple reported that one-third of its sales that first year were to first-time computer buyers. Less than a year later Apple introduced an updated model that came in five bright colors that looked like they came right out of a package of Life Savers. Fierce PC loyalists found fault with the Mac for a variety of reasons, but it didn't matter. In those early days, it felt cool to own a Mac. The "experience" was definitely worth it.

The same goes for hotels. They're fine as long as they're safe and clean while being used for their intended purpose, right? Not exactly. As someone who has traveled more than 200 days per year for more than 20 years, I can tell you that there's a world of difference between a 1-star hotel and a 5-star hotel. In other words, it's all about the experience.

My experience with a 1-star hotel usually began at the front door, which was actually two sets of doors, the first of which would allow me but not my luggage into the vestibule where I now had to open a second set of doors to the lobby. Meanwhile the outside door was rapidly closing on my suitcase, which I was pulling behind me. Get the picture?

Finally, I wrangled my bag inside the hotel where I had to check in with the front desk person, who was also trying to answer the phone, which had been ringing off the hook. After being instructed that my room was on the second floor, I discovered that there was no elevator. Most of the time these hotels were in neighborhoods that were good to sketchy.

Now let's say I booked a room at a 3-star hotel. There my experience began with revolving doors that allowed me to effortlessly enter the hotel with my luggage at the same time. A small front-desk team would greet me, while a primary hotel operator intercepted incoming calls. I was also asked if I'd like help getting my luggage to my room. If I declined, I was told where to find the elevator. This time around the location I'd chosen was good to central.

Now let's compare these two experiences with that of a 5-star hotel. The first noticeable difference was that a doorman would rush out to the curb to open my car door and offer to retrieve my luggage and park the car for me. Team members were dressed in formal uniforms. The front desk was well-staffed and singularly focused on my experience, getting me checked in and acquainted with the hotel grounds, often providing a map. My bags were already on a trolley that was on its way to my room, giving me plenty of options. I was free to go to my room or walk down to the beach or have dinner or stop at the bar for a drink. Location? Amazing.

Today it's all about the experience for me. I love TED Talks. I've even had the opportunity to be a TEDx coach for two speakers, so I was fascinated when I saw a TED Talk about designing experiences to be as good as sex. The speaker stressed the importance of designing things that excite all of our senses at once, something that only sex is able to do at the same time. Sight, sound, touch, smell and taste are all engaged when we have sex, and the experience is profound.

So what can you do to make your experience more like sex? Think about the hotels again.

- **Smell** What does a 1-star hotel smell like compared to a 3-star or 5-star hotel? I'd venture to say that 1-star hotels smell like cleaning products at best. A 3-star hotel smells like good coffee or a pool, while a 5-star hotel smells like fresh flowers or the beach.

- **Touch** What does the bed feel like? At a 1-star hotel, it's probably hard or lumpy with two pillows. At a 3-star hotel it's probably comfortable with three to five pillows. At a 5-star hotel, there's probably a pillow-top mattress, luxurious sheets and five or more pillows.

- **Sound** What does the hotel sound like? At a 1-star hotel, you're likely to hear cars passing by on the highway or noise coming from the hall or the room next to yours. At a 3-star hotel you might hear neighborhood noise. At a 5-star hotel, you'll sleep like a baby since the windows are soundproof.

- **Taste** What's there to eat? If you're at a 1-star hotel, you'll probably have to walk to the nearest minimart. If you're at a 3-star hotel, there's room service until a certain hour and a restaurant on the premises. If you're at a 5-star hotel, you've got your choice of room service 24/7 or an onsite restaurant with an award-winning chef in charge.

- **Sight** How does it look? At a 1-star hotel, things like drinking cups are wrapped in plastic and the towels are stiff and paper-thin. At a 3-star hotel, there's probably a coffee maker in the room and a nice looking lobby and restaurant. At a 5-star hotel, there are fresh flowers in the lobby, friendly staff members are there to help, and your room is so beautiful that you'll be tempted to take pictures and post them on social media. In her book, *Simply Sophisticated: What Every Worldly Person Needs to Know*, author Suzanne Munshower wrote that you can tell you're in a great hotel when the flower arrangement in the lobby is taller than you are. Keep that in mind.

So what experiences are you creating and how do they engage all five senses? It's something to think about.

#11 IF YOU ARE NOT CRASHING YOU ARE NOT GOING FAST ENOUGH

I got this idea from watching Anne Abernathy, a luge athlete from the United States Virgin Islands, who at 53 was the oldest female athlete to compete in the 2006 Winter Olympics. Abernathy was sponsored by the Red Hat Society, an organization founded in 1998 for women age 50 and over, which meant that lots of people had a real interest in how she would perform. In an interview I saw, Abernathy admitted that she got very upset and even felt defeated when she crashed. Her fear of crashing became such a problem that she was not being competitive enough. In other words, she was being too careful.

One day her coach told her, "If you are not crashing, you're not going fast enough." That idea really resonated with me, and since that time one of my goals in life has been to make as many mistakes as I can once. The challenge with going through life scared of crashing or making mistakes is that you'll eventually miss out on things because the best way not to crash is never to do anything risky. For some people, not taking risks is fine with them, yet without risk, there is very little reward. People who are afraid of crashing because it would mean getting out of their comfort zone and trying something new cannot address the negative things happening in their lives because doing so would require them to do something new.

There are two types of people who crash all the time. What separates them is what they do after the crash. People like Oprah, Abraham Lincoln and Elon Musk turn failure into success, and they don't make the same mistakes twice. Substance abusers or people who get fired for cause over and over again get caught in a cycle of bad behavior that leads nowhere because they keep making the same mistakes.

When I was young I was late for work everyday. It wasn't because traffic was heavy or it had snowed the night before or anything like that. It was because I did not get out of bed in enough time to get the things I needed to get done and make it to work on time. I wasn't just crashing into a tree; the tree I was crashing into was me, everyday. The day it clicked for me was when I realized that my clients were showing up on time to see me and that I was always late for them.

I have had some crazy commutes in my life. One job required a 106-mile round-trip on the New Jersey Turnpike every single day. One commute was 90 minutes door-to-door and involved two trains and a subway. I did this for years and was never late for work once. You see, life is not about getting it right the first time because that only happens once in awhile. Life is about making mistakes and learning from them. Here's what I try to do when I have an unexpected outcome or what I call a learning experience. Think of it as a postmortem; it's just something I make part of my daily life when something happens that I did not expect.

1. What just happened? Review the event and outcome.
2. Was this a good thing to have happen again or did I crash into tree?
3. What can I learn from this outcome that I want to do again?
4. If I crashed, have I hit this tree before?
5. What part of this crash was I responsible for?
6. Am I hitting new trees or just the same ones?
7. What part about this crash was out of my control at the time?
8. Should I try again the same way?

So how do you stop hitting the same trees without letting life speed past you because the brakes are always on? Whenever I have had situations where life was a challenge, it wasn't new crashes that were killing me; it was crashing into the same tree again and again. What I needed was to find a trigger, pattern or reminder that I was about to crash again and was about to see my own skid marks, again, right before I hit the tree, again. I'd like to share two stories with you about the trees I hit when I tried to quit smoking and when I tried to lose weight.

Since it is difficult if not impossible to smoke while cutting and coloring hair, I usually had a cigarette when driving or out socially. In fact, it seemed like my car needed a lit cigarette in order to start. That was a trigger for me, so I would place something in my left hand—the hand I used to smoke—before I went to the car. It might have been a lollipop, a toothpick or even a pen. The idea was to have something to hold other than a cigarette as I learned to make it to my destination without hitting the smoking tree. That simple exercise broke the pattern.

When I was about 32, I picked a number I called my "Oh Shoot Weight." The idea was not to let my weight creep up past that number even if it meant giving up things I love to eat for a while. This was working pretty well for me until about a year ago when I gave up traveling for business. The real downside was that I was no longer running through airports and convention centers, which had enabled me to walk from 15,000 to 20,000 steps per day, something I'd done for 20 years. I was fit because of my job, but once I gave up that life I was just a 50-year-old man working from home, eating three meals a day and recording only about 300 to 1,000 steps a day. I hit the ice cream tree so many times, I thought hitting the popcorn tree might be a better idea. So there I was mindlessly eating popcorn, which I thought of as a healthier alternative to ice cream, every night until I realized that I was just hitting another tree and not losing any weight.

I knew I had to do something to keep from hitting that sitting-in-front-of-the-television-mindlessly-eating tree, and that's when I picked up a guitar. Now instead of mindlessly eating while I watched television, I sat with an unplugged electric guitar in my hands and mindlessly noodled on that. In about a month I was down 14 pounds. Knitting, a stress ball or even a pet might have worked. I just had to find something for my hands to do while I was watching television so I wouldn't hit the same tree again and again.

All of my successful friends have hit a lot of trees in their lives. Some even grow new trees to hit. It's the ones who keep hitting the same tree over and over who have the most challenges in life.

#12 EXCUSES ARE FOR LOSERS

This includes no justifying, denying or laying blame.

The Tortoise and the Hare, one of Aesop's Fables, tells the story of a race between unequal partners. A hare ridicules a slow-moving tortoise, which becomes so tired of the hare's arrogant behavior that he challenges him to a race. The hare quickly leaves the tortoise behind and, confident of winning, takes a nap midway through the race. When the hare awakens, however, he finds that his competitor, crawling slowly but steadily, has arrived before him at the finish line and he has lost the race.

The lesson I like most from this fable is that the tortoise made no excuses. He didn't ask for a head start since he was so much slower than the hare. Instead, he challenged someone he knew would take what he had for granted. Instead of making excuses or worrying about what the hare was doing, the tortoise kept moving forward at a steady pace until he won.

As soon as I hear excuses, I shake my head because the fact is, excuses only make the loser feel better; they don't change the outcome. Let's unpack three of the most popular ways people try to excuse their own behavior:

- **Justifying** The definition of justify is to show or prove to be right or reasonable. In the context of excuses, justifying is used to explain away behavior that resulted in a bad outcome. "You don't understand," someone might say. "If the test hadn't been given in the morning things would have turned out differently."

- **Denying** The definition of denial is the action of declaring something to be untrue. Facts are facts and denying the fact that you were late or not responsible for your actions is a slippery slope in any situation. Of all the excuses, denial can be the toughest to overcome.

- **Laying Blame** The definition of laying blame is to hold someone or something responsible for an outcome. Many times this is a justification after the fact because of bad of even disastrous results. When someone lays blame on someone else, they're usually trying to shirk personal responsibility. Let's say someone says, "If the kicker had not missed the final point we would have won." Even if the kicker had missed the final point, laying blame on him alone discounts the rest of the team and their ability to have scored earlier in the game. The excuse takes away from the truth that the whole team did not score enough points to win before the last kick.

There are a lot of excuses out there that can make us feel better. The truth is, and you can see this from many of the greats in sport, excuses are for losers. When winners don't win, they know that it just wasn't their day, they will take the time figure out what happened and they will be back next time to win.

#13 YOU CAN'T PLAN A GOOD BANK ROBBERY WHEN YOU ARE TOO BUSY ROBBING GAS STATIONS

This quote is from my dad, Patrick J. McIvor, Sr. He used to use that expression when I was young. Now, my dad is not a bank robber nor has he ever robbed a gas station. He actually owned an advertising agency and was Communications Director for Johnson & Johnson in the 1970s and early 1980s. This was actually his disruptive way of saying that you have to take the time to sharpen your tools and pay attention to what's important.

My dad's words have inspired me to achieve goals and take advantage of opportunities that have been presented to me. The moral to his story is that if you are always working hard, yet still living paycheck-to-paycheck just trying to keep up or get by, you don't have the time to create a plan that can help you make all the money you need to be financially secure.

Early in my career I accomplished a lot by working very, very hard and making personal sacrifices to get to where I wanted to be professionally, but I wasn't happy. I was wearing a suit, sitting behind a desk and constantly being contacted by people who needed me to fix things for them, but all I could think was, "How did this happen?" So I quit my job, opened up a small business and took the time to focus on my craft. In less than a year, *Allure* named me one of the best colorists in the country.

My next move was to quit all my traveling jobs, work only four days a week in the salon and make time to study photography, play golf and practice yoga. The result? A team won three awards based on the photographs I took of their work, my business had a waiting list, and I was offered a job managing an entire team at a multimillion dollar salon in New York City. As you can imagine, my life was about to change again, but I had new skills and tools to work with because I took the time. Because I had proven photography skills and was recognized by a major magazine, big companies wanted me, too.

As I continued to grow I realized that I not only needed to make time to do the things I wanted to do to get better, but that it was also okay to stop sometimes and take time to think about the big picture. Microsoft Chairman Bill Gates used to take a whole week off—he called it "Think Week"—and go into isolation to review new ideas and pore over papers by Microsoft engineers, executives and product managers. These week-long rituals inspired groundbreaking ideas, like Microsoft's Internet browser, Microsoft's Tablet PC and an online video-game business.

I immediately understood how productive a "Think Week" could be, yet who has the time to indulge in something like that? In my case, I was the sole provider for my family, but my wife understood that if I wanted to emulate the behavior of successful people that I needed the time to gather my thoughts and plan for the future. What we came up with was a "Think Weekend."

For so many of us, life seems to be little more than trying to keep up and not do anything wrong. Ever wonder why so many business deals get made on the golf course? It's probably because playing eighteen holes of golf takes time, and in that time you've got the luxury of thinking and planning. CEOs get that. The best advice I can give anyone who's in the rank and file is to take up golf and use the time to plan your next big success.

#14 MONEY IS A TOOL, NOT SOMETHING YOU SPEND

In his book *Rich Dad, Poor Dad*, author Robert T. Kiyosaki makes the observation that money is a tool. Essentially, it's not how much money you make, it's how much money you keep and how you put that money to work for you.

Let's say you won the Mega Millions lottery drawing. What would you do with all that money? Without careful financial planning, statistics show that if you took a one-time payout thinking you'd be set for life, you'll be struggling again within 10 years. Why? People who aren't smart about money spend it on things they don't need or really can't afford—a second home, a fleet of cars, airplanes or yachts. People who aren't smart about money don't realize how much upkeep these kinds of investments require and learn the hard way that they really can't afford the things they paid cash for. Next thing you know, they're broke.

The secret is to have your money make money, turn expenses into investments and only incur good debt.

- **Have your money make money.** The problem with spending your money first is that it's like killing the goose that lays the golden egg. Money invested in an interest-bearing account makes money for you 24 hours a day. The reason rich people stay rich is that their money is making money even when they're asleep. Let's say you had a million dollars earning three percent interest. In a year you'd have an extra $30,000. That's money you made even when you were asleep. Even if you don't have a million dollars, start putting money away now so it can make money for you. Start with all the pre-tax deductions that let you put 100 pennies of each dollar away because no taxes have been taken out yet. Find out what your maximum pre-tax deduction can be for your 401k and take that amount out of each paycheck. Then see what other investments you can make. Whoever invests the most now will have more money to spend later while that money is still making money for them.

- **Make as many expenses you can investments.** What expenses do you have? Let's start with housing, a car payment, a phone, a computer and rent or a mortgage payment on your place of business if you're self-employed. The thing is, these expenses can add up quickly. Most of us pay these expenses after taxes and without any deductions. If you own your own business, many of these expenses can be paid for with pre-tax dollars. Can you afford to buy your own home? If so, it's a good investment because instead of paying rent to someone else, you're building equity and good credit. You can also deduct some or all of the taxes you pay on the property and interest on your loan, which is money in your pocket at the end of the day. If you own your own business, you may be able to deduct everything from a company car to phones, computers, and tablets. Now your phone may be a business investment, not a personal expense. Again, check with your accountant and current tax codes to see what's allowable.

- **Only have good debt.** Credit card interest is always bad debt, while a mortgage or company car can be good debt. A reasonable college loan debt can be good debt if it opens the doors to a good career. Many hundreds of thousands of dollars of college debt may make a good life nearly impossible. Many people who don't currently have any financial means can look at debt and be afraid of all debt, even thinking things like credit cards are bad. So remember, it's hard to be rich if you are afraid of debt and think credit cards are bad. I love charging things I need to my credit card. It's not bad debt because I make sure I have the money saved first, make sure it's something I need and always pay it off at the end of the month. What's more, I earn points or cash back, qualify for higher credit limits and even improve my credit score by using this strategy.

#15 KNOW YOUR BRAND

This is something comedians are very good at while actors, bands and even politicians aren't always good at. A comedian may go onstage and tell his audience, "I'm fat" or "I'm a redneck." They're honest with themselves and their audience, and that becomes their act or their brand. They know that if they are not truthful with their audience and the audience knows it, the audience will turn on them. Could you imagine Jerry Seinfeld trying to be Eddie Murphy or Andrew Dice Clay or Sam Kinison? They were all up-and-coming comedians during the same time period, but for a while it looked like Jerry's brand wasn't going to be that big. *Seinfeld* changed everything. Here's some advice: Unless your brand is literally about change—think Madonna or David Bowie or Lady Gaga—don't change it. Instead, let your brand evolve.

So what is your brand? I like to think that it's you on your best day. It's you on a first date. Anything from your clothes to your glasses to your hairstyle can establish your brand. The all-American girl next door is a brand. Stevie Ray Vaughan's string-bending guitar solos were his brand. Think about the tortoise and the hare again. The tortoise didn't deviate from his brand, he just crawled to the finish line. The hare got distracted. I know a lot of people who are like the hare and become too distracted to become successful with their brand.

So how can you figure out what your brand is? I use a technique that is based on how we learn and absorb information. It starts with our five senses—sight, sound, smell, touch, taste and touch. List those five items on a page and answer these questions:

1. If your brand could be seen, what would it look like?
2. If your brand could be heard, what would it sound like?
3. If your brand was a smell, what would it smell like?
4. If your brand could be tasted, what would it taste like?
5. If your brand could be touched, what would it feel like?

If you are scratching your head right now trying to answer these questions, let me tell you a story that might help. I graduated from high school in 1985. I was that strange, creative kid everyone knew but no one was friends with. In fact, no one signed my high school yearbook. I was the original Duckie Dale from the movie, *Pretty in Pink*. Let's just say that our sartorial styles were similar—a shirt I might have designed and sewn myself, a vintage white tux with tails, ripped jeans, a pink sneaker on one foot and a purple sneaker on the other. I took Ballet, Engine Shop and Sewing as electives in the same year. My last paying job prior to being a hairdresser was working as a mechanic for the New Jersey Turnpike State Police.

So as you can imagine, my hairdresser friends were surprised that I was always working on my antique cars, while my friends at the garage thought it was weird that I wanted to go to beauty school. So now that you know a little bit more about me, here is how I answered the first set of branding questions:

1. **If my brand could be seen, what would it look like?** A kid on Christmas morning opening gifts and tearing through the wrapping paper so all you can see is scraps of paper flying through the air. If you have ever seen me live or on YouTube, you know I have a lot of energy.

2. **If my brand could be heard, what would it sound like?** The sound at the beginning of a TED Talk with the sonic boom and then clapping. I know how to get the attention needed to do good things.

3. **If my brand had a smell, what would it smell like?** Opium Perfume or patchouli oil. Both have very strong, unique scents. Once you have experienced their smell and you know their name, you will recognize them again instantly. The one thing I am not is a light, flowery smell.

4. **If my brand could be tasted, what would it taste like?** A Chai Tea Latte. I'm different, but I'm not that unusual of a taste.

5. **If my brand could be touched, what would it feel like?** A live snake skin. If you rub it in the right direction it is very smooth, but if you rub it in the wrong direction it does not feel real good and does not go backwards well.

So those are the first five branding questions I use to help companies, teams and individuals understand their brand and how others perceive them. The abstract questions are powerful for many reasons. There are no "right" answers. They simply make you think about yourself differently. The way we learn is through our senses after all. When answering these questions, be as specific as possible. If you said your brand tasted like chocolate, what kind? Milk chocolate? Dark chocolate? Godiva or Hershey's? If you said you look like a muscle car ready to take off at the starting line, tell me what make and model. Are you a 1965 Mustang or a 2018 Dodge Charger? Think about how different the décor of a bar would look if it was a muscle car. Adding details like make, model and year brings that picture into sharper focus.

Branding is important, especially if you get it right. Nike makes sense when you understand that the wing in the air or "swoosh" is a nod to the statue of the Greek Goddess of Victory, Nike. How about Apple? You might wonder what a piece of fruit has to do with a computer company. Look closely at the logo. Someone has taken a bite out of that apple, a reference to a half-eaten apple that was found next to Alan Turing's body after his suicide. Alan Turing, of course, was a pioneer in computer science, who developed a machine that helped break the German Enigma code and laid the groundwork for modern computing. Starbucks was a small coffee shop on the Seattle waterfront that took its name from the chief mate in the book, *Moby Dick*. That two-tailed mermaid on its logo merely reinforces Seattle's seafaring history.

When Steve Jobs stepped away from Apple, it became clear that the people who came after him did not understand the brand, which suffered greatly. It wasn't until Jobs returned to Apple that the company was able to right the ship. Some companies grow without understanding that growth will change the brand, not grow it. Coca-Cola learned this lesson the hard way with the disastrous introduction of New Coke in 1985.

#16 BE INNOVATIVE OR DON'T LET YOUR GROOVE TURN INTO A RUT

This is the classic story of love and hate. Let's start with love. An innovative product or idea is fresh or original. An innovative person is someone creative who is constantly coming up with new ideas. When the stars align, people fall in love with the innovation or the innovator, yet that's when things can start to go downhill.

Now let's talk about hate. I'm a pretty black-and-white person, and I have learned that being average is probably worse than having people hate you, not that having people hate me is ever my goal. Think about trends that peak or hot new songs that everyone loves until it reaches a point that they hate them. Have you ever looked at old photos and thought, "What was I thinking?" Still, there are plenty of people for whom fashion missteps and bad hairstyles have become their look. The trick is not to let your groove turn into a rut, yet that can be a double-edged sword just like love and hate.

Being innovative is tricky. Sometimes an idea catches on quickly— from pet rocks to those "invisible dogs" people walked at the Jersey Shore to viral videos. Then, just as quickly, they lose their appeal almost as if they happened by accident.

Some companies try to innovate and realize that they can't or shouldn't. Think about the computer industry in the 1980s. Every company that introduced a new product in those days was innovative. Why? Because the entire concept of personal computers was brand-new so being innovative was in every company's DNA. A few companies, like Apple, were more innovative than others, branching out into music with iTunes and the iPod and then introducing the iPhone, the iPad and now the Apple Watch. Other companies learned very quickly that they just could not innovate far beyond the personal computer and that no one was interested in their mp3 players, tablets and cell phones. For those companies, the mistake was getting stuck in their groove. The customer wants innovation, not a copy of something that was innovative.

There are two reasons why things fail. One is that they don't change. The other is that they change too much. The secret is to figure out which is right for your brand. I've always preferred evolution to change. I created something I call my Concrete Branding Exercise. When you complete the exercise at the back of the book, you will notice that your brand falls into one of three main categories: Consistent, Pragmatic or Experimental.

To make this easier to understand, I've provided examples of brands that fit into each of these categories.

- **Brands That Are Built on Consistency and Stability**
  (Concrete Branding Exercise: Consistent)
1. Magazine or TV Channel: *Organic Living* and *Parents* magazines, Golf Channel
2. Car or Mode of Transportation: Volkswagen Beetle, Harley Davidson
3. Band or Musician: Wayne Newton, Brittany Spears, Bruce Springsteen
4. Designer, Label or Store: Tiffany, Burberry, J.Crew
5. Celebrity or Person: Anna Wintour, Christie Brinkley, Cindy Crawford, George Clooney, Oprah

- **Brands That Constantly Make Some Changes**
  (Concrete Branding Exercise: Pragmatic)
1. Magazine or TV Channel: Network television, ESPN
2. Car or Mode of Transportation: Corvette, Mercedes-Benz
3. Band or Musician: Coldplay, U2
4. Designer, Label or Store: Target, Levi Strauss, Calvin Klein, Converse
5. Celebrity or Person: Beyoncé, Jennifer Lopez, Sarah Jessica Parker

- **Brands That Make Wild Changes and Don't Repeat Success** (Concrete Branding Exercise: Experimental)
1. Magazine or TV Channel: *Visionaire* magazine, Netflix, Amazon, iTunes

2. Car or Mode of Transportation: Uber, Lyft, Zipcar

3. Band or Musician: Pharrell, Jack White, Zedd

4. Designer, Label or Store: Marc Jacobs, Christian Siriano, Kilt

5. Celebrity or Person: David Bowie, Lady Gaga, Madonna

The irony is that all three of these categories can be the key to success and the key to failure. What matters is whether or not the brand understands who they are, what their customers want and who their customers are. The only brands that win when their customers grow old are eldercare and the funeral industry. For every other brand, it's important to appeal to new customers as their original customer base ages. The winners are the ones who are paying attention and know where their next audience is coming from.

"Okay" has never been good enough for me. Finding my groove made me successful, but not letting myself get into a rut has allowed me to stay there. I have two tattoos: an arrow pointing forward on my left wrist and a star on my right wrist. Because I am left-handed, I see that arrow more frequently, and it always reminds me that I need to keep moving forward. The star on my right wrist reminds me to keep my feet on the ground and to keep reaching for the stars. They are my reminders each and every day to innovate and don't let my groove turn into a rut.

#17 BEING THE BEST
DOESN'T EVEN COUNT

Remember when being the best counted for something? *He's my best friend. This is the best day ever.* Yet, it's often difficult for people to articulate what being the best actually is. The truth is, the "best" is usually just the most popular choice, right now.

Businesses often use the word "best" to describe their goods. There is a scene in the movie *Elf* where Buddy, the naïve elf who travels to New York City in search of his real father, takes his street-smart girlfriend on a date, surprising her with a cup of "The World's Best Coffee" while she tries to explain that it's just marketing.

You've probably heard of Ichiban, a chain of Japanese restaurants with locations all over the United States. "Ichiban" literally means "best" in Japanese. Can you imagine a restaurant that called itself Best? No. Yet here's a restaurant that managed to do just that, albeit in a foreign language.

In my life I have also learned that being the best has its downside. Where do you go from there? I was born in New York and grew up less than an hour away. I spent the majority of my career working as a hairdresser in Manhattan where I managed departments generating millions of dollars in revenue or led artistic teams for major hair and beauty manufacturers. You know what you don't want to be in New York City? You don't want to be the best because chances are that you will be knocked off your pedestal in a New York minute. Case in point: What was the hottest ticket on Broadway before *Hamilton*?

New York City is the most competitive market in the world. From fashion to finance, food to entertainment, it's the place to be if you want to be the best. The city attracts tourists from all over the world who want to eat at the best restaurants or see the best Broadway shows. Performers dream of playing Madison Square Garden or Carnegie Hall. Everyone from chefs to stockbrokers, hairdressers to musicians, goes to New York City to be the best. What many of them do not know, often until it is too late, is that you can get burned when you fly too close to the sun. Think of Icarus, the son of the famous craftsman Daedalus in Greek mythology, who taught his son to fly with wings he fashioned from feathers and wax. Despite his father's warnings, Icarus flew higher and higher, ultimately flying too close to the sun, which melted the wax and dissolved the wings, plunging him into the sea where he drowned.

The reality is that it's easier to be the best in smaller or less competitive markets. Maybe you're the best colorist at the small salon in your hometown. The question is, are you good enough to qualify as an assistant for the best colorist in New York City? In other words, the definition of what's the best is constantly changing depending on the context. For example, you could be the MVP for a AA Minor League Baseball Team, but you may never have what it takes to be moved up to a AAA Minor League Baseball Team let alone find yourself playing in the Major Leagues.

When someone tells me that I'm the best, I take that as my cue to get back to working my butt off.

#18 IT'S NOT IMPORTANT WHAT YOU DO; WHAT'S IMPORTANT IS THAT YOU CAN DO SOMETHING BETTER THAN OTHERS

I learned early on that it is not important to be well rounded or good at everything. In fact, when I was young I struggled in school trying to get the kinds of grades my parents and teachers expected of me, and it was difficult for me to just sit still and listen. Today I'd probably be diagnosed with ADHD, but who knew about those things in the early 1970s? Let's just say that because of my poor grades and general disruptiveness, my parents and my teachers got to know each other very well.

By second grade, concern about my educational wellbeing was mounting, and my maternal grandmother, Carmella Ferlauto, decided to get involved without telling anyone else in the family. In order to motivate me to do better, she offered to pay me to complete a specific assignment. It was a series of 26 worksheets, and she promised to give me $5 for each one. Imagine my seven-year-old self being offered an opportunity to make that kind of money. Needless to say, I accepted her offer.

So one day my second-grade teacher was going through my very messy desk when she discovered a number of my friend Steven's worksheets there. Naturally, she called my mother, and the two of us had to meet after school so I could explain why my very smart friend's completed worksheets were in my desk. I came clean, of course, and told them everything. I'd come up with what I thought was a foolproof scheme: pay Steven $2 for his worksheets and still turn a profit of $3. I guess I was outsourcing long before I knew what the term meant. What strikes me as surprising now is that I don't remember being punished for my behavior. My grandmother found herself in hot water with my parents, but when it came to me, maybe they just threw up their hands and decided that I was resourceful enough to make a living and they didn't have to worry about me. So I wasn't good at everything, but I was good at one thing: making money.

I think being well rounded can hold people back from being better at one thing than everyone else. There's a book by Tom Rath called *Strengths Finder* that I love. He talks about focusing on our strengths rather than trying to be great at something you might never be anything but good at. He uses Michael Jordan as an example. By most accounts, Jordan is the greatest basketball player of all time, but he also excelled in a few other sports (he had been a pitcher at Laney High School in Wilmington, North Carolina), and it had long been a dream of his to play professional baseball. So on October 6, 1993, Jordan announced that he was leaving The

Chicago Bulls. On February 7, 1994, he signed a minor league contract with the White Sox. As it turned out, Jordan was not as adept at hitting a baseball as he was at dunking a basketball. Once he realized that and took up basketball again, he returned to being the best at one thing.

People call themselves specialists for a reason. The word itself is defined as "a person who concentrates primarily on a particular subject or activity; a person highly skilled in a specific and restricted field." There's a difference between a diner and restaurants that specialize in certain types of cuisine. A Spanish tapas bar, for example, has become very good at one thing, while a diner tries to be all things to all people.

So many people today fail to realize that being good at a lot of things might mean you are not great at anything. The truth is that we all have greatness in us. Some of us have found what that is and some of us are still discovering what that is. In his book, *Good to Great: Why Some Companies Make the Leap and Others Don't*, author Jim Collins examines the reasons for why some companies defy gravity and convert long-term mediocrity into long-term superiority. One of his conclusions is that good is the enemy of great because for most of us, "it is just so easy to settle for a good life." My advice: Don't settle.

#19 BE PROFESSIONAL, ALWAYS

This is a lesson that too often is learned the hard way.

The definition of professionalism is "competence or skill expected of a professional." Someone who is unprofessional exhibits behavior that is below the standards expected in a particular profession. So what makes people behave unprofessionally in the first place? It's been my experience that pure ignorance is often to blame. If no one has told you what the standards of practice and ethics for a particular field are, how can you be faulted for not knowing them?

So if no one has ever given you a roadmap for acting professionally, here is my advice:

1. Don't intentionally try to make anyone angry.
2. No naked pictures on social media.
3. Avoid politics, religion and sex in casual conversation with clients or in the workplace.

4. Make it your responsibility to know what is expected of you as a professional in your chosen field.

5. Make it your goal to find ways to exceed professional expectations.

6. Look around and see what other professionals have done that impresses you.

7. Ask yourself one question: "Will this come back to haunt me?"

Finally, it's easy to underestimate the impact that personal appearance can have on how we are perceived. Could you imagine getting on an airplane and feeling confident if you saw the pilot wearing a wrinkled shirt and no name tag on his or her jacket? Frankly, that would alarm me even though it seemingly has nothing to do with their ability to fly the plane.

Five Things a Professional Needs to Do At All Times

1. When getting dressed in the morning be prepared or leave enough time to make sure you are looking your best that day.

2. Be where you need to be at least 15 minutes early; otherwise you're late.

3. Look people in the eye. Say "please" and "thank you." Acknowledge the good others are doing and graciously accept acknowledgement from others.

4. Even when things don't go as expected, make sure you were giving 100%.

5. Create time and space for you to let go and just be you. What happens in Vegas doesn't stay in Vegas anymore. It lives online forever. So don't think that getting your freak on and posting it might not affect your profession or your personal life.

#20 READY, FIRE, AIM

Most entrepreneurs who go into business for themselves can't afford to fail. So how do you find out what works and what doesn't? It's been my experience that most people fail because they failed to try, not because they tried and failed. There are numerous examples of people who became the best in their industry only after trying the most, failing the most and adjusting their **aim** the most. Top sales people learned from the no's they got. Top tech start-ups, skateboarders and snowboarders learned from planning (**ready**), trying (**fire**) and making adjustments (**aim**). Most people are so worried that they won't hit the bull's-eye on the target, while successful people know that they are probably not going to hit the bull's-eye. They're just trying to hit the target to see where they are. This is how the gun is sighted.

Rifles have a telescopic sight on top called a scope that provides an accurate aiming point. The scope needs to be sighted in order for the crosshairs—the aiming device used inside most popular rifle scopes—to work. Rifles need to be sighted every time they are used since any sudden jolt or movement can knock the rifle out of alignment. So how do you sight a gun? First, you have to set up a rifle rest that keeps the rifle from moving during the sighting process. Then set up a target with a bull's-eye at 25 yards. Most rifle sighting is done first at 25 yards, then at 100 yards to provide an accurate sighting over long distances. Check the scope to determine if the crosshairs are lined up with the bull's-eye. Then you use a three-shot process to sight the scope, making adjustments as necessary. What's important to remember is that it's not the gun that's adjusted, it's the sights, and you don't know how to make those adjustments until you fire the gun.

Here's how I apply the concept of sighting a rifle to my life. Before I try anything new, I look around to see if there is anyone I think has less natural ability than me who has done the same thing successfully. When I realize that if they can do it, I can do, I'm **Ready**. Then I look around to see what else I should do to be ready. Can I just take a lift to the top of a mountain and ski down or do I need to prepare by taking a class or observing other people do the same thing? When I make a decision, I'm ready to **Fire**. The key here is confidence. Don't try to hit a home run your first time at bat. Instead, be aware of what you are doing or trying to do and fire. Then I look to see how I did. In other words, what was the outcome? If I was close, I make minor adjustments. If I was way off target, I make major adjustments to my **Aim**.

A couple of years ago the TED Radio Hour featured Tim Harford, an economist and journalist who wrote a book about failure. Harford told an interesting story about Unilever's attempt to design the perfect nozzle for creating powdered soap. The company actually solved the problem by creating 10 random variations on the nozzle. They tried out all 10, kept the one that worked best and repeated the procedure until they created one nozzle that truly hit their target. This story proves the point that there are plenty of cases where failure is an option.

#21 FIGURE OUT WHAT YOU HAVE TO DO IN ORDER TO DO WHAT YOU WANT TO DO

Rules are a fact of life, but not all of us are rule followers by nature. When I was young I was a bit of a handful. By the time I was in seventh grade, I'd been removed from two schools for general disciplinary problems. One of those incidents happened in third grade when I actually organized a school gang complete with laminated membership cards, ranks and code names. Doing what people wanted me to do was a challenge because what they wanted me to do never seemed to be the thing that I wanted to do.

I always loved to work. Before I was old enough to have a newspaper route of my own, I filled in for other paperboys when they went on vacation or had other commitments that prevented them from completing their route. When I was old enough, I got two paper routes. Before I was 17, I found a way to earn money by washing dishes, bussing tables, mowing lawns, shoveling driveways, making salsa at a Mexican restaurant, working at a tree nursery, sweeping floors at the YMCA and being a guard at an ice skating rink. I got most of the jobs I applied for. I guess if I'd done what I needed to do I would have gotten the others as well, but I made a different choice. Whether it was good or not, I learned something from each experience.

The High-End Restaurant

I bought my first car when I was 17. That meant that I had to pay for car insurance, gas and upkeep, and that required money. I grew up in an upper-middle-class neighborhood in New Jersey during the 1970s and '80s, and working at a high-end banquet restaurant that hosted a lot of bar mitzvahs was the place to work if you wanted to make real money. The parties they catered there were as over-the-top as you could get without offending grandparents and grandchildren. I remember wheelbarrows filled to capacity with shrimp. I have never seen the amount of shrimp I saw at these bar mitzvahs than anywhere else, even on a cruise ship. When I filled out my application, I had no reason to believe that I wouldn't get the job. I'd gotten every other job I applied for, and I was a good worker. As far as I was concerned, it was in the bag.

I wore a jacket and tie to my interview with one of the managers. Things were going well when she told me that I would have to remove my earring in order to work for them. Imagine the sound of brakes locking up on a car so it loudly skids to a stop. That's the sound I heard inside my head when she made that request. I politely told her that removing my earring was not an option for me since I had fought to get permission from my family to pierce my ear, and I withdrew my application. Was that the right choice? I'll never know, but I'm happy with the outcome even though I would have made a lot more money working at a high-end restaurant than minimum wage, which was $3.35 at the time.

The Shoe Store

I was already working as assistant manager at a men's clothing store in our local mall when I applied for a part-time job at a shoe store a few doors down to get more hours. I happened to be friends with the manager, who assured me that the job was mine if I wanted it; I just had to take a test. I had never taken a test for a job before, and this one was unlike any test I'd ever taken. The test consisted of various scenarios designed to test your loyalty? Critical thinking? In one scenario, I was asked what I'd do if I saw an older employee taking money from the safe every Tuesday and returning it on Friday. My options were: A) Tell the manager; B) Tell the police; C) Tell the employee; D) Nothing because he always put the money back every week. I might have chosen A or C if he wasn't returning the money, but given the facts I had, I chose to be compassionate and picked D. I finished the test, choosing to be compassionate more often than not. Needless to say, I flunked the test and did not get that job. In retrospect, I'd have to say that it was their loss, not mine.

My First Corporate Job

As I got older I discovered that I might have to do things I really didn't want to do so that I could do something I really wanted to do. My first corporate job is a good example. I had never worked for a big company, yet I got hired by one of the biggest hair care brands in the world when I was just 21 years old. Up to that point

I'd managed to get by using my ability to talk to people. I guess you could say that I'm a natural-born storyteller. Oral presentations were easy for me; writing wasn't. In fact, writing papers and paperwork in general were right up there with going to the doctor for a round of shots as a kid.

I was one of six team members, who worked remotely in the field teaching and supporting distribution, and at our first meeting with my boss I learned that paperwork was an important part of my new job and that the company respected employees who took it seriously. Submitting your paperwork late was frowned upon so I had to make it a priority to get my paperwork in on time, no exceptions. What I learned was that the better I looked on paper, the more things I could do. For example, when I wanted to put a regional artistic team together, I put my ideas in writing and submitted them to my boss.

Every company I have ever worked for has different things that are important to them or their company's culture. Maybe it was being on time for meetings or events. One company mandated that I wear a watch. Standing, clapping, dancing and high-fives were an integral part of trainings at one company I worked for. At the time this was new to all of us and quite intense, perhaps too intense for some people. At one training I was at, one of the team members announced that he was going to the bathroom. He never returned. Later we found out that he'd gone to the front desk, checked out of the hotel and gone home. I remember thinking, "I didn't know that was an option." Apparently it wasn't because the director of the event told us that the defector would be informed that he was no longer part of the team. That's when I realized that being a team player was a cardinal rule in this new world I'd entered and that opting out of anything was simply not in my best interests.

Years later at a very long and exhausting training, a group of junior educators was sitting together in the theater. Some of them were clapping, but most of them were joking around with each other. Someone had taken a video of the group, which we were shown the next day. Members of that group were asked to stand and explain what they were doing. "Is that how a leader leads?" they were asked. The obvious answer was, "No."

I've been on teams where I was expected to wear business attire. I've also been on teams where flip-flops were perfectly fine. What's important is that you know the rules and play by them. If you are looking to be a success in a particular company, see what kind of behavior other people are being corrected for and make sure you aren't doing that. Learn from others what you need to do and do those things perfectly. Then don't ask for permission and work hard to do the other things you want to do.

#22 DON'T BE NICE, BE HONEST

Frankly, nice people aren't the ones who will tell you that you have lipstick on your teeth. Nice people won't be the ones to tell you that your zipper is open. They'd rather pretend they did not notice any of these things instead of running the risk of embarrassing you. I've got an acronym that works here:

N (Nothing)
I (In Me)
C (Cares)
E (Enough About You to be Honest)

I've discovered that people who are nice to me don't care as much as the people who are honest with me, yet fair. I want people around me who will help me see things I didn't notice but need to know. I don't want them to be mean, but if my favorite shirt should be retired, I'd rather they told me. Don't make me wait until I look like one of those people who end up on a show like *What Not to Wear.*

If a friend needs to lose or put on a few pounds, if he has bad breath, if his comb-over isn't working, if his eyebrows are scary or he needs to switch to a stronger deodorant, I hope he'd want me to be honest with him so he can make adjustments. It's not to be mean; it's because not telling him about these things would prolong the situation or make it even worse.

I want to know that I am surrounded by people who are comfortable enough with me to be honest when I need to hear it. I respect people who understand this and don't use it as an excuse to be mean. I don't need people who can't be honest on my team, but they can sit in the audience.

#23 NINE TIMES OUT OF TEN
THE PROBLEM IS ME

The one thing all my problems have in common is me. In fact, it is the only thing all my problems have in common.

The problem with problems is that other factors always come into play. The way I look at my problems is to assess the situation to determine what factors were in my control. There is always a choice I made that contributed to the situation I find myself in, but the question is, "What do I do about it?" If it's important, I always "pack my own chute."

Everyone has problems. There's simply not a person alive who will not run into problems at some point. Still, we all handle problems differently. Let's look at some of the ways people address problems when they arise.

Some People Solve Their Problems

These people in life are winners. Winners are not winners because they have no problems; winners are winners because they understand that problems are going to occur and that they may, in fact, be part of the problem. These people figure out how to fix the problem and, more importantly, keep it from happening again. Their mantra could be the expression, "Be part of the solution, not part of the problem."

Statistically people we view as winners may have more misses than hits, more failed attempts than successes. We see it all the time in athletics, art, music, literature and business. In fact, I know two types of successful people who have had more negative than positive outcomes, yet they were able to learn from their mistakes. Certainly, skateboarders and snowboarders learn from their mistakes. Tony Hawk learned from the mistakes he made creating amazing new tricks on his way to becoming a skateboarding legend.

Professional poker players know that to become rich you only need to win every third hand. Annie Duke, a professional poker player and author, who holds a World Series of Poker gold bracelet from 2004, knows a thing or two about that. Her autobiography, *How I Raised, Folded, Bluffed, Flirted, Cursed and Won Millions at the World Series of Poker* was published in 2005. After years of playing poker, Duke realized that there's no point in trying to create luck. Her advice is to seek good advice, weigh the odds and get everything to go your way. A few years ago Duke discussed making big decisions in the face of great uncertainly with CNBC contributor Don Schawbel, suggesting that while even champions are likely to lose a lot of great hands in poker, the important thing is to learn from the outcomes. "Venture capitalists spread their bets among a bunch of these long shots, creating a basket of high volatility, high potential return investments," she told Schawbel. "They know that any single investment is likely to fail, but the basket of investments will likely win."

Some People Make Their Problems Worse

Many times these people see themselves as victims of their problems. They might try to explain how the problem began and what they did to make it better. Sometimes they exacerbate their problems by trying to hide what happened in the first place. Think about someone who gets caught in a lie and instead of coming clean tells another lie. Now their problem is even wore because they have one more lie to cover up. The poet Sir Walter Scott said it best: "Oh! What a tangled web we weave when first we practice to deceive."

The bottom line is that if you recognize that you have a problem and you are not able to be part of the solution, understand that you are most likely going to make the problem worse. The thing is, your problems don't define you. We all have problems. The trick is to accept the fact and make peace with it.

Some People Are Their Own Worst Problem

People whose biggest problem is themselves fall into one of two categories: those who are enabled and those who are self-destructive. Let's say that your biggest problem is that you're a food addict. We've all watched those reality shows where someone who is grossly obese has been confined to bed and can no longer leave the house. Chances are that someone compounded the problem for one reason or another, in effect enabling them.

Now think of the alcoholic who goes to rehab only to relapse again and again. This kind of self-destructive behavior is inevitable unless they learn from their mistakes.

I can be my own worst enemy when I'm triggered by things like long lines, large crowds or situations in which I'm with people 24/7. These things can become overwhelming at which point I need time alone to regain my equilibrium. So I've learned to let people know upfront that if I get some time alone they'll like me better.

#24 BE 100% COMMITTED

Being less than 100% committed to any undertaking, even if it's by only one percent, is already a gamble and could make the difference between a good outcome and a great one.

What is 100%?

Have you ever watched footage of an elite athlete or star compete or perform as a child and later as a teenager and young adult? Then you've probably noticed that while they gave 100% each and every time, they kept getting better. Some people think that once they've given 100%, they have no more to give, but that just means they have no more to give right now. Sometimes we are just not at 100%, but that doesn't mean we can't still bring 100% to what we're doing.

Professional athletes know that better than anyone. Manchester City goalie Bert Trautmann finished the 1956 FA Cup with a broken neck. Gymnast Kerri Strug vaulted to a Gold Medal on an injured ankle in the 1996 Atlanta Olympics. Michael Jordan scored 38 points with the flu in Game 5 of the 1997 NBA Finals.

So what exactly is 100%? For me it's giving 100% of what I got right now.

No Backup Plan

For some people, having a backup plan seems like a good idea because it dispels the negative emotions associated with taking a risk, but new evidence shows that having a Plan B might actually set you up for failure. In a story for *The Washington-Post* in 2016, Ana Swanson wrote that "merely contemplating options other than success can make your goals harder to achieve." Her conclusions were based on studies conducted by the Wisconsin School of Business at the University of Wisconsin-Madison and the Wharton School at the University of Pennsylvania, which showed that those who made backup plans were hobbled by a "diminished drive for success."

I pursued hairdressing as a career while also going to college. I went to college because I liked to learn, period. College was never a backup plan. I was 100% committed to making it as a hairdresser, and I did. I have always believed that anyone who dips their toes into life will never have the success they dream about. Greatness is achieved by those who left themselves no other option.

Seeing It Happen

Believing you can do it is powerful, and visualizing yourself doing it is proven to be even more powerful. Think about martial artists who breaks a brick or block of wood with their bare hands. Before they could break that brick or board in two, they had to visualize themselves doing it. Pitchers who can visualize themselves throwing a perfect game by internalizing the images and seeing their own success have a huge advantage over everyone else. It's like the thing they want to accomplish has already happened, giving them up to a 30% advantage over their competitors who hope to accomplish the same thing.

One thing I've learned is that it doesn't matter what other people think. It only matters what you think. People who believe they can't do something are probably right. It's like a self-fulfilling prophecy. My wife always asks me why I find it necessary to plan out every detail before executing an idea, and I tell her that it's because I have to see something being successful before I start.

My mother always encouraged me to risk everything as long as I didn't go into debt. I think that's pretty good advice. I like to try new things all the time just to see what will happen, but I've learned not to do anything unless I'm 100% committed and can visualize myself being successful. Too many people fail because they don't know what 100% commitment looks like. When I need a refresher course, I surround myself with five people I know who get it. That's how I stay focused.

#25 THERE AIN'T NO TRAFFIC
ON THE EXTRA MILE

The difference between being good and great can be infinitesimal. Take the athletes who compete in Track and Field at the Olympics. The difference between winning a gold, silver or bronze medal in the 100 meters might be as little as one hundredth of a second. This is clearly where going the extra mile separates the legends from everyone else.

Companies that go the extra mile earn customer loyalty and increase business. Casey Bunn, CEO of Handsocks, which makes cozy mittens for babies and toddlers, sends a note to everyone who buys his product from Amazon to make sure they are completely satisfied with their purchase. In 2017 he began collecting stories about actual children and named a limited edition collection of mittens after them. San Francisco-based Kimpton Hotels started a program for guests who are traveling alone on for business and miss their pets. Upon request, a goldfish will be delivered to your room to keep you company. The staff takes care of the actual upkeep. All you have to do is enjoy it.

Celebrities like Ed Sheeran or Lady Gaga have made names for themselves by going the extra mile for fans. It turns out that being approachable and, well, just plain nice, can be good for your career. Captain America Chris Evans, in full Marvel costume, and Chris Pratt (*Guardians of the Galaxy*) visited sick kids at Children's Hospitals in Seattle and Boston after the Super Bowl in 2015. German musician Zedd does private, unannounced concerts for his fans, who can win tickets by completing scavenger hunts. Now that's legendary.

For me, going the extra mile means doing something completely unnecessary, yet extraordinarily thoughtful. Certain charities go the extra mile by treating the community they serve with respect. I'm thinking of organizations like Dress for Success, which provides professional attire and a network of support to empower women to achieve economic independence. The Dress for Success boutiques don't look like second-hand stores. Instead, women browse through racks of shoes and clothing that are attractively displayed. Think high-end boutique, not thrift store.

At 16 I knew that it was important to respect yourself first and be as respectful as you can to others. Going the extra mile is nothing more than a demonstration of respect, while also exceeding expectations. What I love about going the extra mile is that it doesn't have to cost money. It just takes a little time. Once I make the decision to be thoughtful, going the extra mile is easy. There's nothing standing in my way. Like I said, there's no traffic on the extra mile.

CONCLUSION

Many cultures celebrate a young person's transition from childhood to adulthood with some kind of ceremony. Sweet sixteen parties have been a coming-of-age tradition in the United States and Canada for years. Latinos have traditionally marked a girl's 15th birthday with an elaborate party called a *quinceanera* or *fiesta de quince anos*. In China a hair-pinning ceremony marks a girl's eighteenth birthday. These rites of passage are designed to encourage young people to ponder their lives as adults. This book began as a conversation I had with my daughter Emma when she was 16, but the truth is, it's a conversation I wish someone had had with me when I was trying to figure out what I wanted to be.

When I was 16 years old I wanted to be an Army Ranger and study law. I vividly remember going to the career center at my high school to look into colleges. After answering a series of questions, I was told that The American University of Beirut in Lebanon was a good fit for me. Ultimately I didn't go to college there or join the military or study law, but I did a lot of other things—some on purpose, some by accident—that led to success and financial security. Looking back, I wish that when I was 16 I had known that what mattered wasn't what I wanted to *be*—an Army Ranger, an attorney—but that I needed to surround myself with successful people doing what I wanted to do.

At 51, my 16-year-old self is a distant memory, but I still make sure that the five people I spend most of my time with make me want to be a better person. They might be smarter than me, more successful than me or more courageous than me, but they always inspire me to make a difference, aim higher, do more with my life.

We frequently travel with our daughters. They've been to London, Paris, Dusseldorf, Rotterdam, Amsterdam, Turks & Caicos, Prague, Vienna and Budapest. I have created jobs for myself in a variety of ways—opening salons, coming up with unique positions within corporations, writing blogs and, now, publishing this book. I have never had credit card debt. I learned to love good debt by purchasing my first home when I was just 26 years old. I have put money away every year and watched it grow.

Aside from the fact that almost everything that I know I learned from someone else, it has always been experience that has kept me from making the same mistakes twice. And while I have never thought that I was better than anyone else, I know that I'm one of the luckiest people on earth.

One thing I learned from my parents was how to create an experience. My father used to do amateur magic shows, and we went on family vacations to far-flung places like San Francisco and Jamaica. The object was to visit places that were very different from where I grew up so early on I knew what a great experience

107

feels like. I've been a hard worker my entire life, always hustling to make a buck. I knew money was a tool I could use to build wealth, and I took the time to create jobs that would fill my bank, not just my tank.

The power of a moment is that it is right now and it is unique. It's unlikely that this exact moment will ever occur again. We each have 86,400 seconds a day to create the life we want. Personally, I want to live them to the max, fully committed to being there. When we are not 100% committed to doing the things we have to do, we may end up complaining all the time and making things worse. I can think of three situations in which being less than 100% committed can have a drastic outcome.

Driving a Car
Texting while driving can have deadly consequences if you are distracted for even a fraction of a second.

Snowboarding
In this sport you have to pay strict attention to what you're doing. Because of the way your foot is strapped onto a snowboard, you don't want to look in any other direction than where you want to go. Start looking at that tree over there and you are probably going to hit that tree.

Floating in Water

If you relax you float; if you panic you sink. So concentrate, relax and float. If you are not 100% relaxed, you won't float.

For me the extra mile has always been *my* finish line. It didn't matter if I finished first, second, third or last. I never stopped when I could; I always went that extra mile. The funny thing about going the extra mile is that when you get up a little earlier than most people and stay a little later, you make things better for everyone. Some people hit the snooze bar on their alarm every morning and complain all the way into work about the traffic they would have avoided if they just got up a little earlier. I have found that creating an extraordinary life that I love is up to me. No excuses and no need to win the Lottery. I just need to do about 25 things right.

Concrete Branding Exercise

1. If Your Brand Was A Magazine, What Magazine Would It Be?
2. If Your Brand Was A Car, What Car Would It Be?
3. If Your Brand Was A Musician or Band, What Musician or Band Would It Be?
4. If Your Brand Was A Fashion Designer or Label, What Fashion Designer or Label Would It Be?
5. If Your Brand Was Embodied or Exemplified By A Person Who Would That Be?

When you get this exercise done you should be able to picture the person, if living, driving up in the car, listening to the music, wearing the clothes and reading the magazine. When done right these 5 concrete places can be used to inspire your brand and its experience with new ideas that make sure your groove doesn't turn into a rut.

ABOUT THE AUTHOR

Patrick McIvor is an internationally recognized hair colorist who has held leadership positions with companies like Redken, Matrix, Wella, Clairol and Goldwell. As an educator and motivational speaker, he has traveled to more than 15 countries and five continents. In 2016 he was invited to share his message about the importance of touch on the TEDx stage. Patrick lives in Nazareth, Pennsylvania, with his wife and daughters.

Made in the USA
Monee, IL
27 January 2020